Oodie
the Donkey

Copyright © 2018 Amy Ekwegh. All rights reserved.
First paperback edition printed 2018 in the
United Kingdom
A catalogue record for this book is available from
the British Library.
ISBN 978-0-9934611-9-4
No part of this book shall be reproduced or transmitted in
any form or by any means,
electronic or mechanical, including photocopying,
recording, or by any information retrieval
system without written permission of the publisher.
Published by Scribblecity Publications
For more copies of this book, please email:
amyekwegh@gmail.com
Printed in Great Britain

Although every precaution has been taken in the
preparation of this book, the publisher and
author assume no responsibility for errors or omissions.
Neither is any liability assumed for
damages resulting from the use of this information
contained herein.

*Dedicated to my goddaughter
Adaugo Isobel Nwogu*

"No! I don't want to go to the field," Dodie moaned.

"It's a beautiful day and the fields are green," said Ruby.

"Don't forget that lovely, cold lake you love sipping water from," Sim added.

"I don't want to be bullied by Storm!' Dodie confessed.

Suddenly everyone became very quiet. Dodie was scared of Storm. Storm picked on Dodie in the school playground, on the field and even at the lake. Storm always said nasty things to Dodie because he was different.

Dodie was the smallest donkey in his class. He also had dark spots and tiny little legs. If only he could change his body into something more muscular.

"We promise to stop Storm from bullying you," Ruby assured him.

"Yes," Sim nodded.

"Okay," Replied Dodie.

He really didn't want to miss the
afternoon fun. It was a hot
day, and lots of foals were outside playing
on the field.

"Let's race to the field," Ruby
shouted as he sprinted off. His friends
raced after him.

"I love the sun!" Dodie exclaimed, as he
stood at the top of the slope gazing at the
glowing fiery ball in the sky.

"It is a lovely day," he added, with a big smile stretched across his face.

The field was filled with lots of foals. Dodie was happy to be out on the field. He didn't care about Storm anymore. He only wanted to have a good time with his friends.

"I am super excited about the festival!" Ruby declared excitedly to his friends.

Everyone in the village was getting ready for the 'Festival of Young Donkeys', which was only a few days away.

It was a festival where every
donkey in Grade 2 would be
presented at the village square and the
best donkeys would be bought.

The little donkeys in the field were very
excited and were looking forward to
this spectacular day.

Before the festival, most donkeys
would stay away from the hot sizzling sun
to avoid getting a wrinkly fur.
Others would apply lots of ointments
to make their coats shine.

The richest merchants always
chose the best
looking donkeys.

"I wish a rich merchant would choose me,"
said Sim.

"Me too!" Dodie and Ruby chorused.

They chuckled as they raced up and down
the slope.

After a while Storm, the bully and his friends appeared from behind the bushes. They started to laugh and make fun of poor Dodie.

"Look at that ugly donkey. He can't even climb!" Storm mocked

"His tiny legs will soon break," another scoffed.

Dodie stopped racing. He was hurt by their words. "Stop being mean to Dodie." Ruby defended his friend.

"Woahh!" The mean group giggled.

"Let's get out of here," Ruby motioned to his friends, Dodie and Sim.

"Hey Sim, why don't you come over and join the champions instead?"

"Buuu-uut," Sim stuttered.

"Come on Sim, you don't want to bruise your coat. The festival is in a few days." One of them waved to him to come over.

"I'm sorry, I really want to look good on the day." Sim mumbled sheepishly as he joined Storm's group.

"Come on, Let's go, champions!" Storm trotted off. His friends quickly followed him.

"I never want to be his friend ever again!" Dodie cried. He was shocked and hurt. How could Sim have left his best friends for a group of bullies?

Dodie, Ruby and Sim had been friends for a long time. They went to school together, played every afternoon together and even shared snacks with each other.

"I can't believe Sim has betrayed us," Dodie wailed.

"We'll always be best friends forever." Ruby assured him.

Dodie was up at the break of dawn. It was the day of the festival and he wasn't feeling happy.

Dodie's stomach churned nervously at the thought of the event ahead. He tried so hard to be positive, but he just couldn't.

I'm scared. He whimpered . "I know I will never be chosen because I'm too weak and ugly!"

"Don't say that! You are not weak and ugly, you are beautiful just the way you are."

Dodie was startled as Ruby appeared from behind the trees.

"O, I didn't know I was speaking out loud."

Dodie stammered, feeling very embarrassed.

"We're going to have a good day, you'll see," reassured Ruby.

"I'm scared. I couldn't even join the birds to sing for luck today." Dodie cried.

"Come on Dodie; let's go wash in the stream. We need to look good." Ruby dashed off before Dodie could say a word.

Before long, the two friends were both laughing and splashing in the cool water.

The day of the festival finally came. Dodie's heart pounded as he stood next to his best friend. He wasn't paying attention to the ceremony.
This was meant to be the best day of his life. Yet, he couldn't stop himself from hearing Storm the bully's scornful voice: "You're ugly Dodie."

"Your legs are frail, Dodie." He could imagine Storm teasing him.

The applause from the crowd brought Dodie's mind back. People were cheering at the soldiers who had just performed.

"That was amazing!" Ruby cheered.

"What?" Dodie couldn't believe he had missed the whole show.

"I can't believe you missed the soldiers' parade!" Whined Ruby.

It was rare to see the soldiers have a march past in the square. They only ever performed at special occasions. The soldiers wore shiny outfits and marched in unison.

"Dodie, you need to relax and enjoy this day. You may not get this opportunity again!"

It didn't take long for the trumpet to sound. The grand finale was near. This was it. It was time for the donkeys to march in front of their buyers.

"Get Set!" One of the soldiers bellowed loudly to the donkeys. Dodie felt like he was going to faint. He was now breathing so fast that his knees felt weak.

"Go!" The soldier roared. Ruby smiled at him and nodded.

At this point Dodie knew it was too late to turn back.

"One, two. One, two." At the command of the soldier, the donkeys began the parade. With heads held high and tails in the air. They looked very smart.

They threw their left legs forward first, then the right. "Left, right, left, right. "After the parade, the donkeys stood in the middle of the square waiting eagerly for the verdict.

Finally, it was time for the men to choose. The king was the first to select three donkeys. "I would like to be a royal donkey," Ruby whispered to Dodie. "Me too!" Replied Dodie.

Dodie wondered who the lucky donkeys would be. If only he would be chosen by the king, but how would the king pick such a weak looking donkey like him.
He thought sadly.

The villagers cheered as the chosen donkeys followed the king's guards.

The donkeys were marching past when a familiar voice whispered, "You're ugly, Dodie." Dodie looked up and saw Storm. He disliked Storm even more for being picked by the king.

How could anyone pick a bully like Storm? Dodie thought.

Sim had also been picked by the king too. He marched past Dodie and Ruby, pretending not to know them. Dodie couldn't believe his friend had changed. He was happy that he still had Ruby as his best friend.

He wished they would be picked by the same Master. Unfortunately, the City's richest tailor picked Ruby.

"Never mind, Dodie, I'm sure someone will pick you very soon." Ruby consoled his friend as he followed his new owner.

Dodie began to shake in fear as everyone walked past him. No one wanted him. Poor Dodie. He felt rejected as he watched the people leave. The square was now empty.

All the other donkeys had been chosen. All gone to their new homes.

He closed his eyes and tried not to cry as he bowed his head in shame.

Storm was right afterall.
The little donkey thought to himself sadly.

"I want... him." Dodie heard a man's voice. His heart leapt with joy. At last someone wants me. Maybe I'm not that ugly.

He didn't feel rejected anymore. He imagined himself in the courtyard of a rich merchant, adored by the children and being fed lots of food.

The touch of his new master on his shoulder woke him from his day dream.

As Dodie looked up at his master, he was filled with disappointment at the sight of the old man.

He didn't look rich like the other men. His hair and beard were grey and bushy, while his robe looked worn and smelt of smoke which tickled Dodie's nose.

I am ugly and frail! Just like the old man. Dodie said to himself as he followed his new master.

The thought of Storm and the bullies laughing at him brought tears to his eyes. Storm was right about him.

Dodie wished Ruby was there to comfort him. How he wished he had sang with the birdies that morning. He tried to hold back a tear from trickling down his face.

The journey to his master's place was longer than he thought it would be. The old man lived on the outskirts of the village.

When they got to his master's little hut, Dodie was tied to a tree beside the hut.

I'm sure Ruby is having a good time at his new home, he thought. Dodie couldn't bear to think about Storm's new home. His master's little hut was nothing compared to the king's palace.

It was a royal tradition for the king to present donkeys to his children after each festival, and all the donkeys would dream of being the chosen ones.

Grrrhhh! Dodie's belly rumbled. His new master must have forgotten to feed him.

He missed his little home. He always had food to eat even though his parents were gone. His mother was taken away by strangers when he was a baby, and his father died few months before the summer.

He wished he could break loose from the ropes and run back to the village.

"Hello, little frail donkey." A young boy came out of the hut. He stroked Dodie's ears. Dodie wanted to tell him not to call him little and frail because it reminded him of Storm, the bully.

The boy brought some food to him and Dodie ate hurriedly. Even though the hay was a bit hard, he was still grateful for the food.

Weeks had passed since Dodie moved to his new home. He really missed his village, and playing in the green fields with his best friend.

He was tied to the tree all day, and had no company except for his master's son who fed him daily. He was bored of watching other donkeys trot by with their owners.

"Ugly Dodie." A familiar voice cut through Dodie's thoughts. It was Storm.

"I told you no one would pick you!" He mocked, as he trotted past with the prince on his back. Storm had the royal trappings around his neck, and his coat glowed.

Dodie buried his head in shame at Storm's words, until he heard footsteps approaching him. I don't want any more embarrassment, he said to himself.

Two men stopped right beside him,
but Dodie still didn't look up. Dodie's
Master spoke with the men who began to
untie Dodie from the tree.
Finally! Dodie thought.

He saw that the man holding his rope was
not his master. Who's this? He thought to
himself, while looking at his master who
was standing behind the two men.

I've been sold by my master.
The thought that even his master no longer
wanted him, made him very sad.

His new owners didn't look rich, but he
was glad to move away from the tree.
He didn't want to be made fun of by
the other donkeys.

He gladly followed the men as they
travelled back to the village. Maybe he will
see his best friend Ruby again.
Dodie thought to himself.

As they got closer, Dodie could see a lot of
people gathered near the
village square.

Before Dodie knew what was happening, he was carrying a man on his back.
For the first time in weeks, he lifted his head and shoulders in pride.

The moment was magnificent for him, because it was his first experience of being ridden. All the practice on the fields and during the parade were not in vain. His legs were able to carry the weight.

Dodie began to follow the leading of his new master as they rode towards the village square.

As they drew nearer, Dodie became
confused because people were
throwing their clothes on the ground for him
to step on. They were also waving palm fronds
and shouting
"Hosanna!"
"Hosanna! All hail the king!"

The closer they got, the more people bowed
before Dodie's master.

I'm carrying a king! Dodie thought to himself.
But who is this king?

"Hosanna!" People continued to shout as they
knelt down by the two sides of the road.

Dodie saw the rich merchants; princes and their donkeys bow down too. It didn't take long before Dodie spotted Storm bowing down with his master.

Dodie's head rose even higher as he took slower strides. I'm a royal foal! I'm unique! He smiled as he looked at Storm who bowed his head in shame. Sim was bowing down too.

People from neighbouring villages joined the crowd as the news about this special King spread. This parade was more special than the royal guard parade.

"Prince Dodie!" Ruby, his best friend, shouted from the crowd.

Dodie turned and smiled at his friend who was also bowing down with his master. Everything seemed like a dream to him.

"You're royalty, Dodie." This time the voice wasn't distant. It was soft and close to his ears. It was his new master.

"How do you know my name is Dodie?" He asked his master.

He smiled. What a beautiful smile,
Dodie thought.

"You are special, Dodie. You are handsome and strong." Responded the master.

For the first time in Dodie's life, he believed he was significant and
special. He didn't care about Storm.

He didn't care about the other donkeys. He was happy with who he was.

"Who are you?" He asked.
"I am the King of kings," His master replied.

"And I am Dodie, the Royal donkey!" Dodie chuckled.

GLOSSARY

Bellow To shout in a loud voice

Festival A special event

Frond Leaf-like part of a palm tree

Hosanna Used to express adoration, praise or joy

Magnificent Beautiful

Merchant A trader or seller

Tradition Beliefs passed from generation to generation

Trappings	An ornamental covering or harness for a horse
Unique	Being different
Verdict	A decision made after judgment
Whimper	small weak sounds expressing pain
Whine	To make a long, high, sad sound

CROSSWORD PUZZLE

```
A C E G  H C S  C R
L B G N  O B X  W E
H C R I  M Z N  O L
K M L H  E M T  E A
J S I T  K X C  T X
K D A O  S P O  R T
L D R L  Q Y T  M M
D Q F C  P B V  L O
T V D P  A R A  D E
```

Frail   Sport   Home   Relax
Parade   Clothing

MAZE

HELP DODIE FIND HIS FRIEND

SPOT THE DIFFERENCES

Can you find the 5 differences in these pictures?

1. Dodie's missing spots. 2. There are two clouds. 3. The man in the green has a missing ear. 4. The tail end of the rope is missing. 5. There is an extra rock.

www.ingramcontent.com/pod-product-compliance
Lightning Source LLC
Chambersburg PA
CBHW070442010526
44118CB00014B/2160